📖 **SCHOLASTIC**

LITTLE LEARNER PACKETS

ALPHABET

Immacula A. Rhodes

Cover design: Tannaz Fassihi; Cover illustration: Jason Dove
Interior design: Michelle H. Kim
Interior illustration: Doug Jones

ISBN: 978-1-338-23029-1
Copyright © 2018 by Scholastic Inc.
All rights reserved.
Printed in the U.S.A.
First printing, January 2018.

4 5 6 7 8 9 10   40   24 23 22 21 20

Table of Contents

Introduction 4–6

   Connections to the Standards 4

   How to Use the Alphabet Packets 5

   Teaching Tips 6

   Assessing Learning. 6

Alphabet Packets

   Packet 1: A, B, C 7–14

   Packet 2: D, E, F 15–22

   Packet 3: G, H, I 23–30

   Packet 4: J, K, L 31–38

   Packet 5: M, N, O 39–46

   Packet 6: P, Q, R 47–54

   Packet 7: S, T, U. 55–62

   Packet 8: V, W, X 63–70

   Packet 9: Y, Z, Alphabet Review 71–78

   Packet 10: Alphabet Fun Pack 79–86

Answer Key 87–96

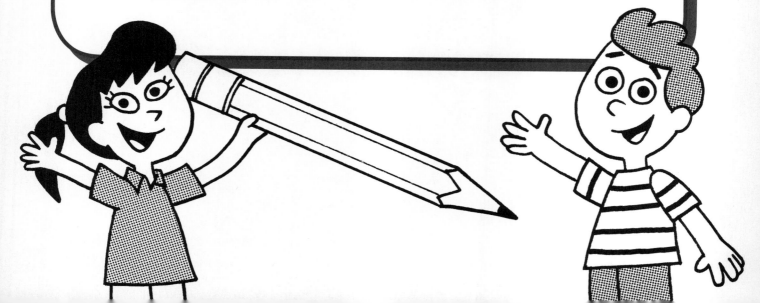

Introduction

Welcome to *Little Learner Packets: Alphabet*! The 10 learning packets in this book provide fun, playful activities that teach and reinforce the letters of the alphabet. The design, organization, and predictable format of the packets let children complete the pages independently and at their own pace—in school or at home.

Each packet targets three letters for children to trace, write, and sequence. In addition to letter formation and sequencing, activities include recognizing, matching, and graphing the uppercase and lowercase letters, identifying words that begin with each letter sound, and completing a color-by-letter picture. A review page at the end of each packet further reinforces the letter skills and can be used as a quick and easy way to assess children's learning.

The final packet—the Alphabet Fun Pack—lets children continue to give their alphabet skills a workout by doing fun activities, such as coloring pictures following a color code, filling in letter sequences, connecting dots to reveal a mystery picture, matching pictures by letter clues, and tracing letter paths. These pages can also be used as fun assessment tools to gauge children's learning. While the packets are designed to boost children's letter skills, the activities also provide lots of opportunities to refine their fine motor and visual discrimination skills.

You can use the packets in a variety of ways and with children of all learning styles. Children can complete the activities at their seats or in a learning center. Or they can use the pages as take-home practice. The packets are ideal for encouraging children to work independently and at their own pace. A grid on the introduction page of each packet lets children track their progress as they complete each page. Best of all, the activities support children in meeting the standards for Reading Foundational Skills for Kindergarten. (See the Connections to the Standards box.)

Connections to the Standards

Print Concepts
Recognize and name all upper- and lowercase letters of the alphabet.

Phonics and Word Recognition
Demonstrate basic knowledge of one-to-one letter-sound correspondences by producing the primary sound or many of the most frequent sounds for each consonant.

How to Use the Alphabet Packets

Copy a class supply of the eight pages for the letter packet you want to use. Then sequence and staple each set of pages together and distribute the packets to children. All they need to complete the pages are pencils and crayons. TIP: To save paper, we suggest you make double-sided copies.

The format of the learning packets makes them very easy to use. Here's what you'll find on each page:

Page 1: This page introduces the letters featured in the packet. Children trace the letters on the page. Then they color in the first box in the tracking grid at the bottom. As they complete each of the remaining pages in the packet, children will color in the corresponding box in this grid.

Pages 2, 3, and 4: Children practice tracing and writing the target letter on these pages. The middle section gives practice in recognizing the beginning sound of the letter in words. At the bottom, children circle the uppercase and lowercase forms of the letter.

Page 5: The top section of this page gives additional practice in identifying the beginning letter sounds of pictures and in making letter-sound associations. At the bottom, children complete each letter sequence.

Page 6: At the top of this page, children use a color code to color the picture. Below, they draw lines to match the uppercase and lowercase letters.

Page 7: Children practice letter recognition and boost early math skills by graphing the uppercase and lowercase forms of the target letters. TIP: Invite children to discuss their results by taking a quick look at the graph.

Page 8: These activities review the letter skills that have been introduced throughout the packet. Children write the letter that represents the beginning sound for each word in the top section.

At the bottom, children fill in the letter to complete each word. TIP: You might use this page as a mini-assessment to check children's progress.

Note that in packet 8, most of the words used for *X* end in that letter sound, instead of beginning with it. In addition, packet 9 features only two letters: *Y* and *Z*. Look for the Review activities for these letters on page 7 of the packet. Then on page 8, you'll find activities that review the entire alphabet. TIP: You can use both of these pages to assess children's letter learning.

Answer Key: The answer key on pages 87–96 allows you to check children's completed pages at a glance. You can then use the results to determine areas in which they might need additional instruction or practice.

Teaching Tips

Use these tips to help children get the most from the learning packets.

* **Provide a model:** Demonstrate, step by step, how to complete each page in the first packet. Children should then be able to complete the remaining packets independently.

* **Focus on the target letter:** Give children practice in identifying each target letter by pointing it out on letter cards and finger-writing the letter in the air. Also, call out words that begin with that letter sound, emphasizing the sound of the target letter in the word.

* **Promote visual skills:** Have children look carefully at the shape and form of each letter. Encourage them to compare letters to identify the similarities and differences in their formation.

* **Give letter-sequencing practice:** Invite children to sequence a series of three letter cards. You might also write letter sequences on the board, leaving out one letter for children to fill in. For auditory practice, say a few letters in sequence, such as *A, B, C.* Then pause to give children time to name the letter that comes next (*D*).

Learning Centers

You might label a separate folder with each child's name and place the packets in the folder to keep in a learning center. Then children can retrieve the assigned packet and work independently through the pages during center time. To make the packets self-checking, enlarge the answer keys for each packet, cut apart the images, then sequence and staple them together to create a mini answer key for that packet. Finally, place all of the answer keys in the center. Children can use the answer keys to check their pages as they complete each packet.

Ways to Use the Alphabet Learning Packets

Children can work through the packets at their own pace, tracking their progress as they complete each page. The packets are ideal for the following:

* Learning center activity
* Independent seatwork
* One-on-one lesson

* Morning starter
* End of the day wrap-up
* Take-home practice

Assessing Learning

The last pages of the Alphabet Packets 1–8, and the last two pages of packet 9 are review pages that can be used to check children's letter learning. The Alphabet Fun Pack (packet 10) also provides a creative way to assess children's skills. In addition, you might do the following to check children's progress:

* Present pairs of uppercase and lowercase letter cards for children to match.

* Call out one letter at a time and have children write the uppercase and lowercase forms of that letter.

* Display two to three letter cards, such as *A, B,* and *C.* Then say a letter sound, for example /b/, and have children point out the letter card for that sound (B).

* Show children a letter card and several pictures. Have them identify which pictures begin with that letter sound.

* Call out a one-syllable word. Ask children to write the letter for the sound that the word begins with.

Name: _MIShKA_

Trace each letter.

Color in each box when you complete the activity.

| ① Introduction | ② Gg | ③ Hh | ④ Ii |
| ⑤ Match & Write | ⑥ Color & Match | ⑦ Graph | ⑧ Review |

Name: _____

Trace, then write.

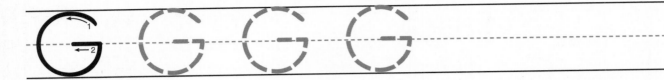

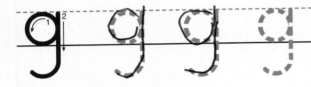

Color each picture that begins with the G sound.

Circle each G and g.

C	g	G	q	G
p	D	g	G	g

Gift!

Name: _____

Trace, then write.

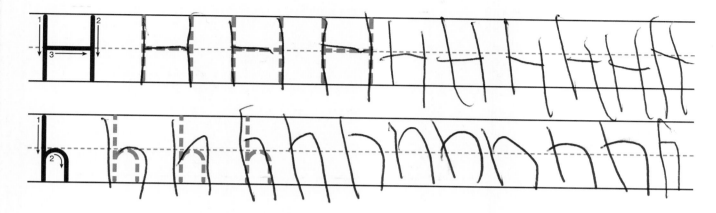

Color each picture that begins with the H sound.

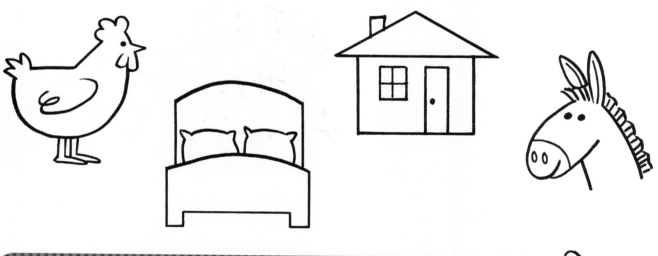

Circle each H and h.

H	k	b	h	H
T	h	H	K	h

Hat!

25

Name: _____

Trace, then write.

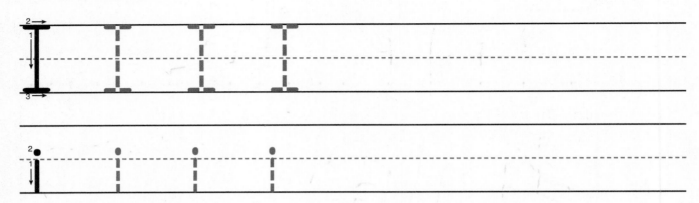

Color each picture that begins with the I sound.

Circle each I and i.

i   J   j   T   i

I   T   I   i   I

Invitation!

Little Learner Packets: Alphabet © Scholastic Inc.

26

Name: _____

Draw lines!

Match each picture to the letter it begins with.

 **Gg**

 **Hh**

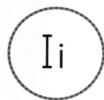 **Ii**

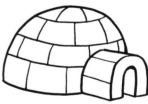

Write the missing letters.

G, _____, I   _____, H, I

G, H, _____   g, h, _____

g, _____, i   _____, h, i

Name: _____

G=  brown   H= blue   I= yellow

Use the code to color the picture.

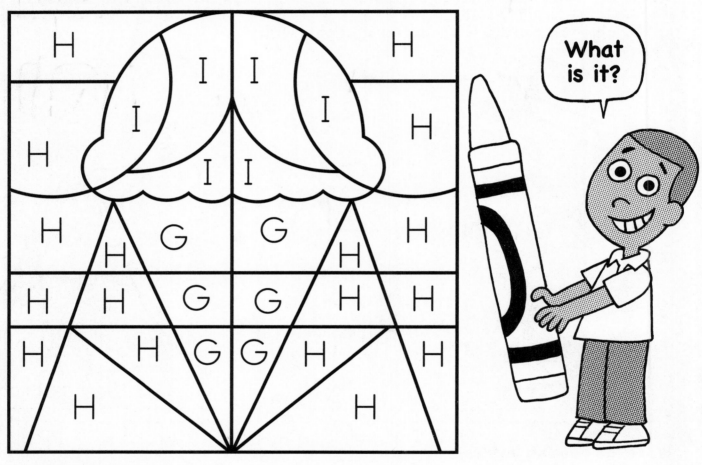

What is it?

Match the letters.

H •   • i   I •   • h

I •   • g   G •   • i

G •   • h   H •   • g

Little Learner Packets: Alphabet © Scholastic Inc.

Name: _____

Count and graph the letters.

g   I   i

G G H h H

H G

I h H I

H g h

Say each letter!

	G	g	H	h	I	i
4						
3						
2						
1						

Fill in the letters. Color the pictures.

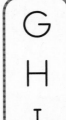

G   H   I

_____ is for  .

_____ is for  .

_____ is for  .

Write the first letter for each word.

g
h
i

 _____en

 _____gloo

 _____oat

Little Learner Packets: Alphabet © Scholastic Inc.

Name: _____

Trace each letter.

Color in each box when you complete the activity.

① Introduction	② Jj	③ Kk	④ Ll
⑤ Match & Write	⑥ Color & Match	⑦ Graph	⑧ Review

Name: _____

Trace, then write.

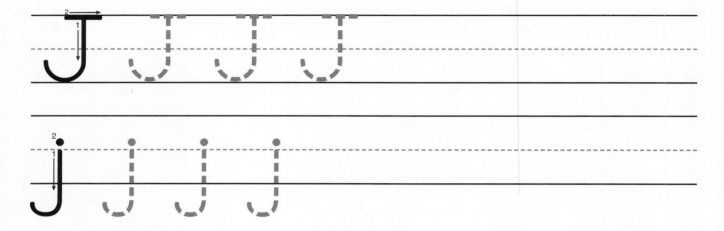

Color each picture that begins with the J sound.

Circle each J and j.

J I j J J

j i T t j

Juggle!

32

Name: _____

Draw lines!

Match each picture to the letter it begins with.

Jj

Kk

Ll

Write the missing letters.

_____ , K, L   j, k, _____

j, _____ , l   J, _____ , L

J, K, _____   _____ , k, l

Name: _____

J=  blue   K= yellow   L= purple

Use the code to color the picture.

What is it?

Match the letters.

L •	• l
J •	• k
K •	• j

J •	• k
L •	• j
K •	• l

Little Learner Packets: Alphabet © Scholastic Inc.

Name: _____

Count and graph the letters.

Say each letter!

	J	j	K	k	L	l
4						
3						
2						
1						

Name: _____

Fill in the letters. Color the pictures.

Great
work!
Bye!

J
K
L

_____ is for  .

_____ is for  .

_____ is for  .

Write the first letter for each word.

j
k
l

____ing   ____eaf   ____et

38

Name: _____

Trace each letter.

LETTERS

M N O

Hi!

Color in each box when you complete the activity.

①	②	③	④
Introduction	Mm	Nn	Oo
⑤	⑥	⑦	⑧
Match & Write	Color & Match	Graph	Review

Name: _____

Trace, then write.

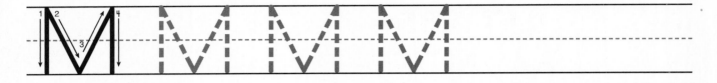

Color each picture that begins with the **M** sound.

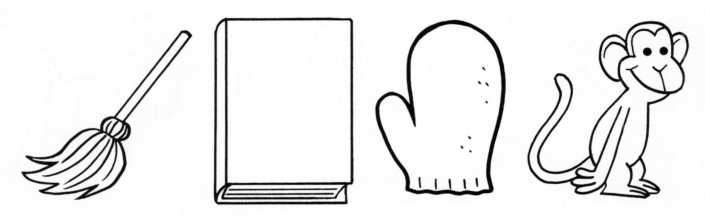

Circle each **M** and **m**.

M   m   W   h   M

m   n   M   N   m

Milk!

Little Learner Packets: Alphabet © Scholastic Inc.

Trace, then write.

N N N N N

n n n n

Color each picture that begins with the **N** sound.

Circle each **N** and **n**.

n   N   H   m   N

M   h   N   n   n

Necklace!

Name: _____

Trace, then write.

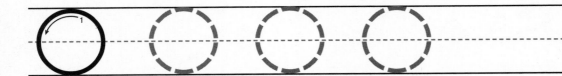

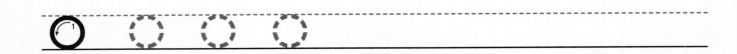

Color each picture that begins with the O sound.

Circle each **O** and **o**.

O a O Q p

o G o O o

Octagon!

STOP

Little Learner Packets: Alphabet © Scholastic Inc.

Draw lines!

Match each picture to the letter it begins with.

 Mm

 Nn

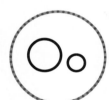 Oo

Write the missing letters.

m, _____, o

M, N, _____

_____, n, o

m, n, _____

M, _____, O

_____, N, O

M = 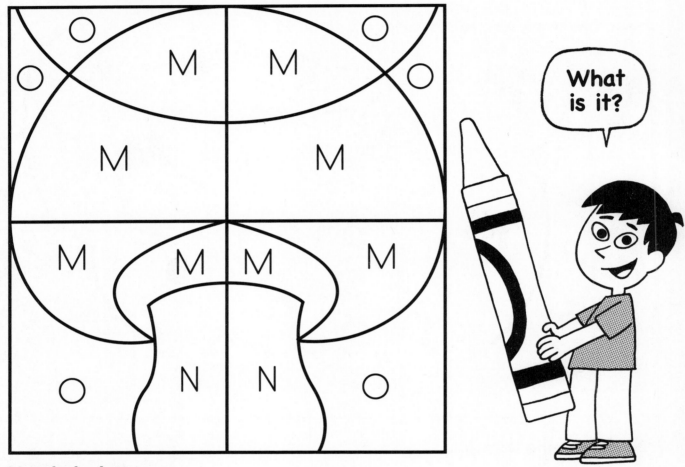 red   N = yellow   ◯ = blue

Use the code to color the picture.

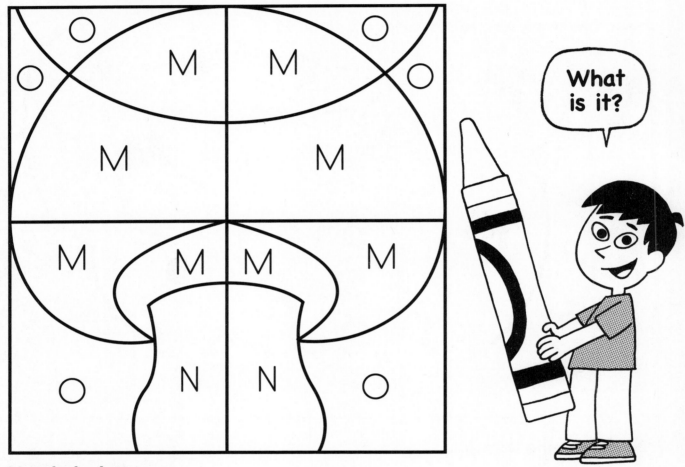

What is it?

Match the letters.

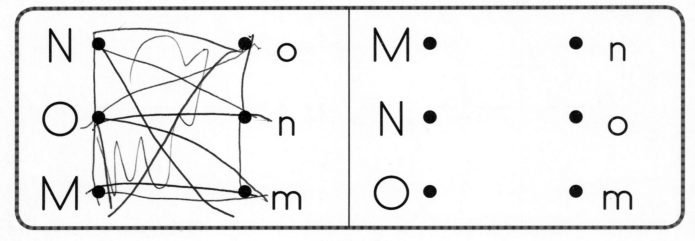

Little Learner Packets: Alphabet © Scholastic Inc.

Count and graph the letters.

Say each letter!

n

m

M o

n o O

N

m M

m

M

o o

O n o

M	m	N	n	O	o
4					
3					
2					
1					

Name: _____

Fill in the letters. Color the pictures.

M
N
O

_____ is for  .

_____ is for  .

_____ is for  .

Write the first letter for each word.

m
n
o

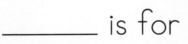

_____live   _____ug   _____ut

Little Learner Packets: Alphabet © Scholastic Inc.

Name: _____

Trace each letter.

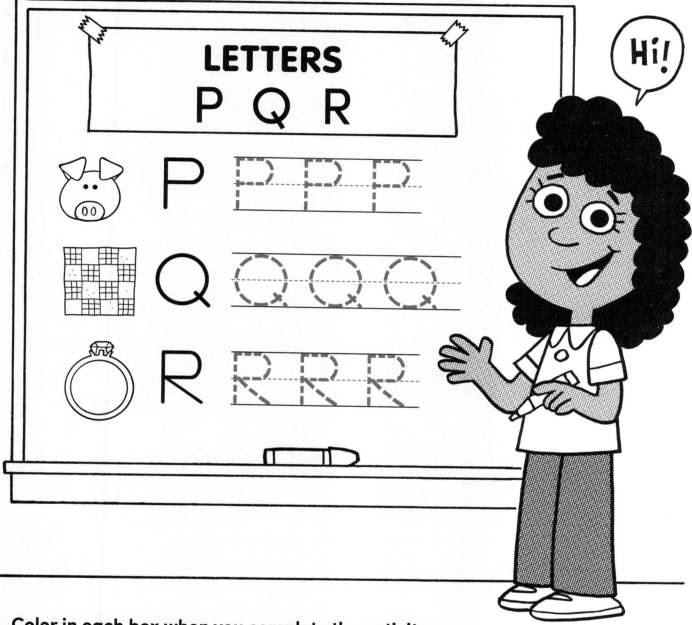

LETTERS

P Q R

Hi!

Color in each box when you complete the activity.

①	②	③	④
Introduction	Pp	Qq	Rr
⑤	⑥	⑦	⑧
Match & Write	Color & Match	Graph	Review

Name: _____

Trace, then write.

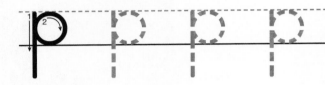

Color each picture that begins with the P sound.

Circle each P and p.

P   q   a   B   P

p   R   P   p   b

Popcorn!

Name: _____

Trace, then write.

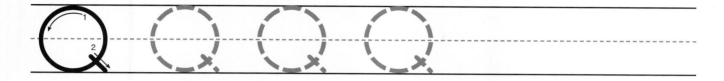

Color each picture that begins with the Q sound.

SHHH

Circle each Q and q.

O	p	Q	q	Q
q	D	q	b	Q

Quarter!

Name: _____

Trace, then write.

R R R R R

r r r r

Color each picture that begins with the R sound.

Circle each R and r.

R P r R r

n R m F r

Rocket!

Little Learner Packets: Alphabet © Scholastic Inc.

Name: _____

Draw lines!

Match each picture to the letter it begins with.

Pp

Qq

Rr

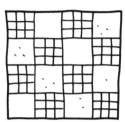

Write the missing letters.

_____, Q, R

p, _____, r

P, Q, _____

p, q, _____

P, _____, R

_____, q, r

Name: _____

P= orange   Q= brown   R= green

Use the code to color the picture.

What is it?

Match the letters.

P •	• q	R •	• q
R •	• p	P •	• p
Q •	• r	Q •	• r

Name: _____

Count and graph the letters.

Say each letter!

	P	p	Q	q	R	r
4						
3						
2						
1						

Little Learner Packets: Alphabet © Scholastic Inc.

Name: _____

Fill in the letters. Color the pictures.

P
Q
R

_____ is for .

_____ is for 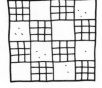 .

_____ is for  .

Write the first letter for each word.

p
q
r

_____ot

_____ake

_____ueen

Little Learner Packets: Alphabet © Scholastic Inc.

Name: _____

Trace each letter.

LETTERS

S T U

S   S S S

T   T T T T

U   U U U U

Color in each box when you complete the activity.

① Introduction	② Ss	③ Tt	④ Uu
⑤ Match & Write	⑥ Color & Match	⑦ Graph	⑧ Review

Trace, then write.

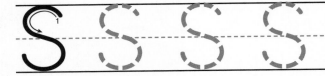

S S S S

s s s s

Color each picture that begins with the S sound.

Circle each S and s.

S	P	s	g	S
p	R	s	S	s

Sandwich!

Trace, then write.

Color each picture that begins with the T sound.

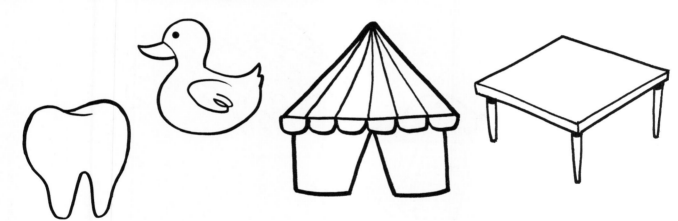

Circle each T and t.

T	k	T	t	I
L	t	h	T	t

Toothbrush!

Name: _____

Trace, then write.

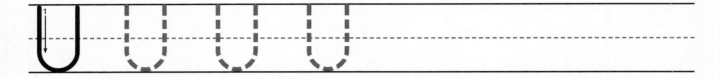

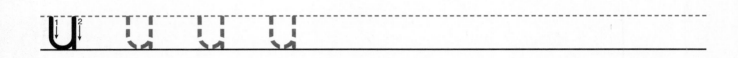

Color each picture that begins with the U sound.

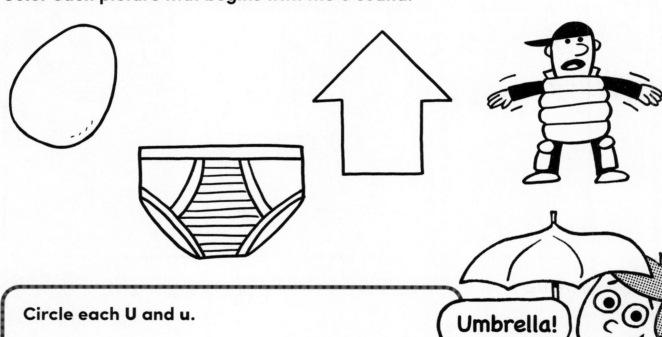

Circle each U and u.

| u | U | V | w | U |
| W | u | U | v | u |

Umbrella!

Name: _____

Draw lines!

Match each picture to the letter it begins with.

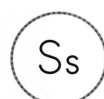 **Ss**

 Tt

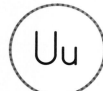 **Uu**

Write the missing letters.

S, _____, U

_____, T, U

s, t, _____

s, _____, u

S, T, _____

_____, t, u

S= yellow   T= green   U= blue

Use the code to color the picture.

What is it?

Match the letters.

U •   • u   S •   • t

T •   • s   U •   • s

S •   • t   T •   • u

Little Learner Packets: Alphabet © Scholastic Inc.

Name: _____

Count and graph the letters.

Say each letter!

T   S
S   u   t   s
S
u
T   t   U   t
S   t   s

	S	s	T	t	U	u
4						
3						
2						
1						

Name: _____

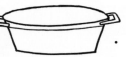

Fill in the letters. Color the pictures.

S
T
U

_____ is for  .

_____ is for  .

_____ is for  .

Write the first letter for each word.

s
t
u

   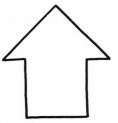   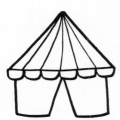

_____un   _____p   _____ent

Little Learner Packets: Alphabet © Scholastic Inc.

Name: _____

Trace each letter.

LETTERS

V W X

Hi!

Color in each box when you complete the activity.

① Introduction	② Vv	③ Ww	④ Xx
⑤ Match & Write	⑥ Color & Match	⑦ Graph	⑧ Review

Name: _____

Trace, then write.

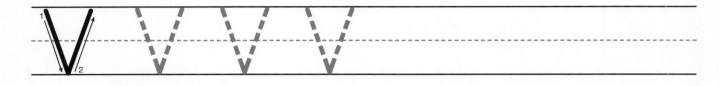

Color each picture that begins with the V sound.

Circle each V and v.

V	k	V	v	V
W	v	A	w	v

Vine!

Name: _____

Trace, then write.

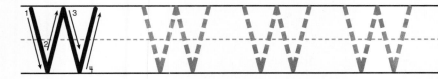

Color each picture that begins with the W sound.

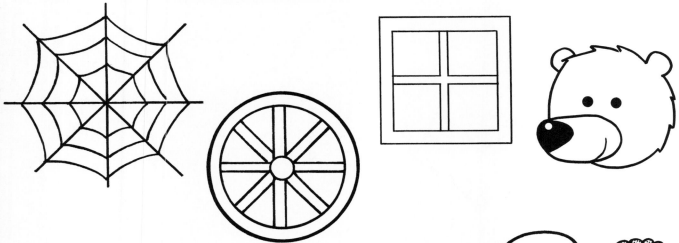

Circle each W and w.

w	W	v	X	W
x	A	w	W	w

Wig!

Name: _____

Trace, then write.

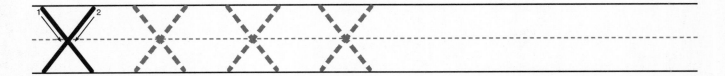

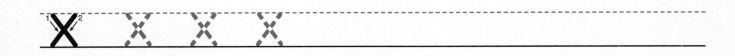

Color each picture that has the X sound.

Circle each X and x.

y   W   X   x   V

X   x   X   w   x

Box!

Little Learner Packets: Alphabet © Scholastic Inc.

Name: _____

Draw lines!

Match each picture to the letter that is in that word.

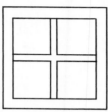

 **V v**

 **W w**

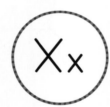 **X x**

Write the missing letters.

V, W, _____ 　　　　v, w, _____

_____, W, x 　　　　_____, W, X

V, _____, X 　　　　v, _____, x

Name: _____

V= brown   W= orange   X= blue

Use the code to color the picture.

What is it?

Match the letters.

X •   • v   W •   • x

W •   • x   V •   • v

V •   • w   X •   • w

7

Name: _____

Count and graph the letters.

Say each letter!

	V	v	W	w	X	x
4						
3						
2						
1						

Name: _____

Fill in the letters. Color the pictures.

V
W
X

_____ is for .

_____ is for .

_____ is for .

Write the missing letter in each word.

V
W
X

_____an

bo_____

_____eb

Little Learner Packets: Alphabet © Scholastic Inc.

Name: _____

Trace each letter.

Color in each box when you complete the activity.

① Introduction	② Yy	③ Zz	④ Match & Write
⑤ Color & Match	⑥ Graph	⑦ Review	⑧ Alphabet Review

Name: _____

Trace, then write.

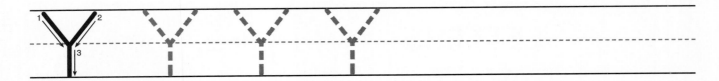

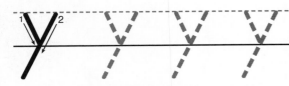

Color each picture that begins with the Y sound.

Circle each Y and y.

Y   v   W   Y   y

y   V   x   y   Y

Yo-yo!

Name: _____

Trace, then write.

Color each picture that begins with the Z sound.

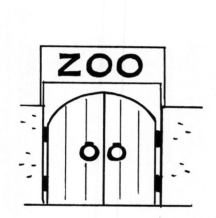

Circle each Z and z.

z   H   T   Z   z

x   Z   z   w   Z

Zero!

Name: _____

Draw lines!

Match each picture to the letter it begins with.

ZAP!

YOGURT

Y y

Z z

ZOOM

Write the missing letters.

X, Y, _____

X, _____, Z

X, Y, _____

X, _____, Z

X, Y, _____

X, _____, Z

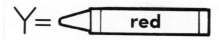 Y= red   Z= blue

Use the code to color the picture.

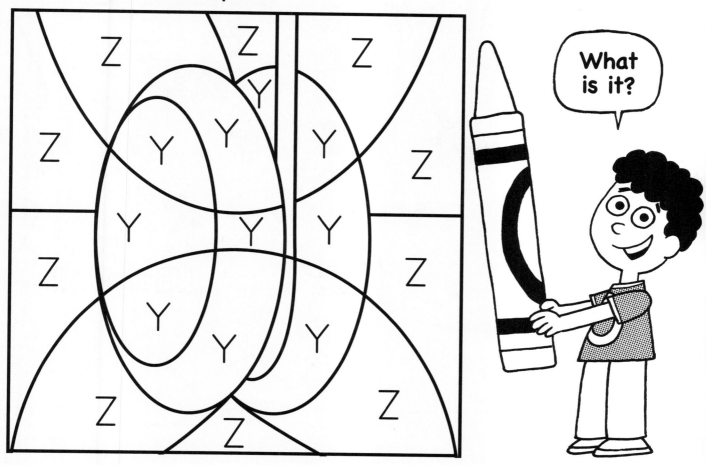

What
is it?

Match the letters.

X •   • z   Y •   • z

Z •   • y   X •   • x

Y •   • x   Z •   • y

Name: _____

Count and graph the letters.

Say each letter!

X	x	Y	y	Z	z
4					
3					
2					
1					

Little Learner Packets: Alphabet © Scholastic Inc.

Almost
done!

Fill in the letters. Color the pictures.

Y
Z

_____ is for  .

_____ is for  .

Write the first letter for each word.

y
z

 _____oo

 _____arn

 _____ip

Name: _____

Write the missing letters.

A, ____, C, D, ____, F,

____, H, ____, ____, K,

L, M, ____, O, ____, Q,

____, S, ____, U, ____,

W, ____, Y, ____

Great work! Bye!

Match the letters.

O •   • q   H •   • n

D •   • r   A •   • a

Q •   • o   N •   • h

R •   • p   V •   • w

P •   • d   W •   • v

Name: _____

Use the color code to color the picture.

A = red   B = blue   C = yellow

D = green   E = orange   F = purple

G = pink   H = brown

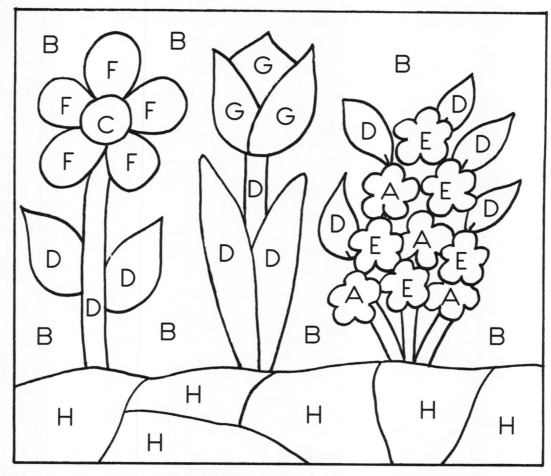

Count the flowers!

Color in each box when you complete the activity.

| **1** Color by Letter | **2** Sequencing | **3** Connect-the-Dots | **4** Trace the Path |
| **5** Connect-the-Dots | **6** Color the Path | **7** Match | **8** Match & Write |

Little Learner Packets: Alphabet © Scholastic Inc.

79

Use my alphabet chart!

ABCDEFGHIJKLM
NOPQRSTUVWXYZ

Fill in the missing letters. Then color the letters of your first name blue.

A _ _ D E
_ G
_ L K _ I
N O _ _ R _ T
_ Y _ W _

Name: _____

Connect the dots. Start at A. Hint: Look for the star.

What is it?

Name: _____

Feed the animals!

Trace the path from each animal to the food that begins with the same sound.

b — b — b — b — e

z — z — e — z — z

l — e — e — l — l — w

e — e — l — w — l

w — w — w

What is it?

Connect the dots. Start at a. Hint: Look for the star.

Name: _____

Color the path from **a** to **z**.

Help me get to my tent!

a b c d e f

r v g

f e h

g j i

k p

l

y u

m n t v

g s f w

d o

r x

p q

d

b v y

z

Match each shoe to its mate.

Draw lines!

SHOE SALE!

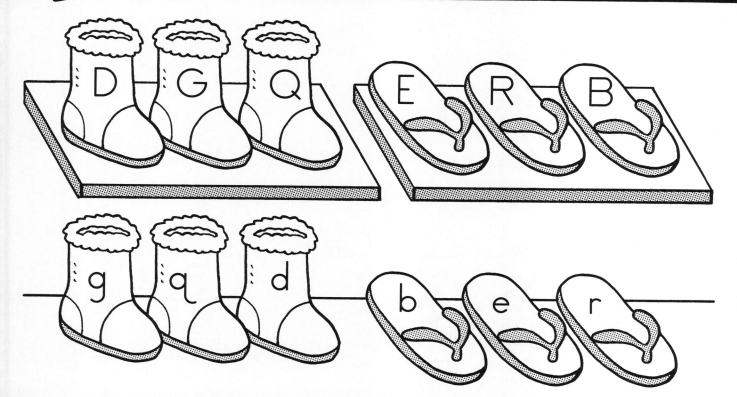

D G Q

E R B

g q d

b e r

J F N

H I L

f j n

l h i

Name: _____

Write the matching letter on each bug.
Use the letters in the box. Then color the bug.

| m | p | s | t | v | w | x | y | z |

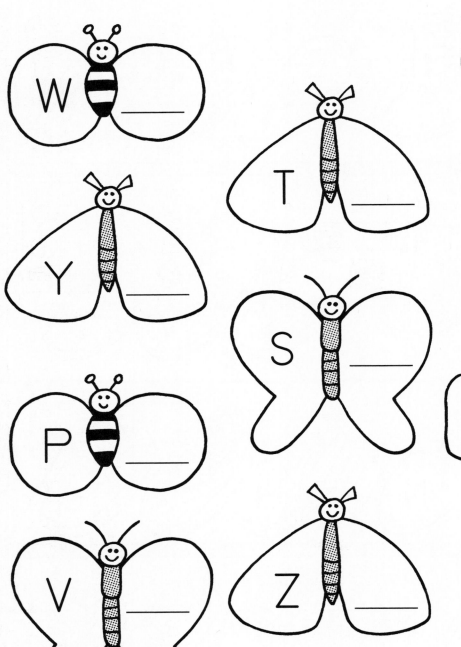

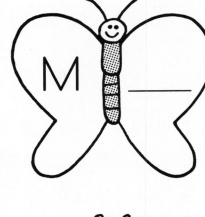

Great
work!
Bye!

86

Answer Key

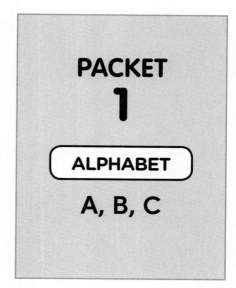

PACKET 1

ALPHABET

A, B, C

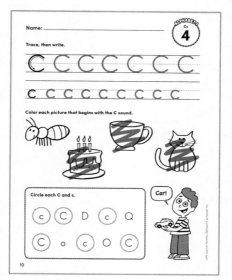

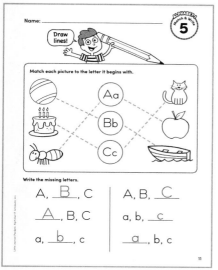

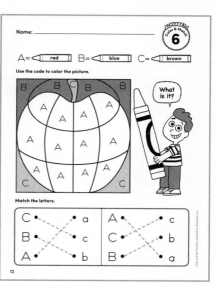

PACKET 2

ALPHABET

D, E, F

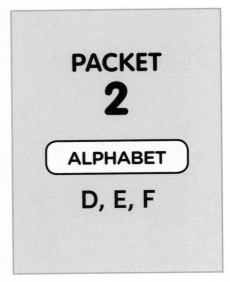

Name: _____

Trace each letter.

LETTERS
D E F

D D D D
E E E E
F F F F

Hi!

Color in each box when you complete the activity.

| 1 Introduction | 2 Dd | 3 Ee | 4 Ff |
| 5 Match & Write | 6 Color & Match | 7 Graph | 8 Review |

15

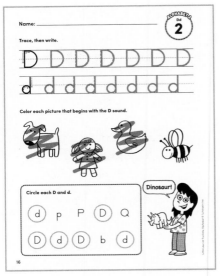

Name: _____

2

Trace, then write.

D D D D D D D

d d d d d d d d

Color each picture that begins with the D sound.

Circle each D and d.

d p P D Q

D d D b d

Dinosaur!

16

Name: _____

3

Trace, then write.

E E E E E E E E E

e e e e e e e e

Color each picture that begins with the E sound.

Circle each E and e.

E F e E c

R e r E e

Elf!

17

Name: _____

4

Trace, then write.

F F F F F F F F

f f f f f f f f

Color each picture that begins with the F sound.

Circle each F and f.

f t f f f

I F E R F

Feather!

18

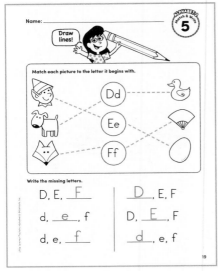

Name: _____

5

Draw lines!

Match each picture to the letter it begins with.

Dd
Ee
Ff

Write the missing letters.

D, E, F   D, E, F

d, e, f   D, E, F

d, e, f   d, e, f

19

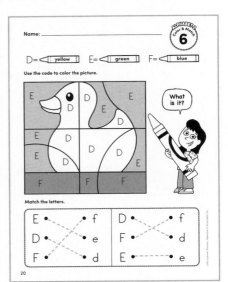

Name: _____

6

D= yellow   E= green   F= blue

Use the code to color the picture.

What is it?

Match the letters.

E • • f   D • • f

D • • e   F • • d

F • • d   E • • e

20

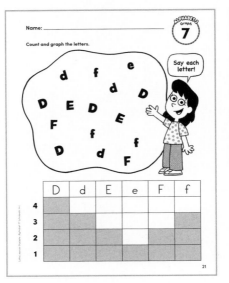

Name: _____

7

Count and graph the letters.

Say each letter!

d f e
D E d D
F D E E f
F f
D d f E

D	d	E	e	F	f
4					
3					
2					
1					

21

Name: _____

8

Great work! Bye!

Fill in the letters. Color the pictures.

D E F

F is for
E is for
D is for

Write the first letter for each word.

d e f

d og   f ish   e lf

22

PACKET 3

ALPHABET

G, H, I

Name: _____

Trace each letter.

LETTERS G H I

Hi!

G GGG

H

I

Color in each box when you complete the activity.

① Introduction	② Gg	③ Hh	④ Ii
⑤ Match & Write	⑥ Color & Match	⑦ Graph	⑧ Review

23

Name: _____

Trace, then write.

G G G G G G G

g g g g g g g g g g

Color each picture that begins with the G sound.

Circle each G and g.

C g G q G
p D g G g

Gift!

24

Name: _____

Trace, then write.

H H H H H H H

h h h h h h h h h

Color each picture that begins with the H sound.

Circle each H and h.

H k b h H
T h H K h

Hat!

25

Name: _____

Trace, then write.

I I I I I I I

i i i i i i i i

Color each picture that begins with the I sound.

Circle each I and i.

i J j T i
I T I i I

Invitation!

26

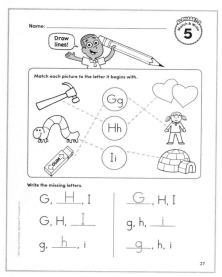

Name: _____

Draw lines!

Match each picture to the letter it begins with.

Gg

Hh

Ii

Write the missing letters.

G, H, I   G, H, I

G, H, I   g, h, i

g, h, i   g, h, i

27

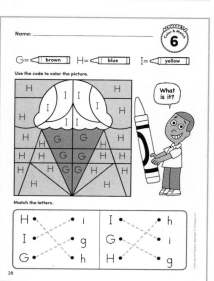

Name: _____

G = brown   H = blue   I = yellow

Use the code to color the picture.

What is it?

Match the letters.

H • • i   I • • h
I • • g   G • • i
G • • h   H • • g

28

Name: _____

Count and graph the letters.

Say each letter!

g I i
G H h H
G
I h H I
H g h

	G	g	H	h	I	i
4						
3						
2						
1						

29

Name: _____

Great work! Bye!

Fill in the letters. Color the pictures.

G H I

I is for _____

G is for _____

H is for _____

Write the first letter for each word.

g h i

h_en   i_gloo   g_oat

30

PACKET
4

ALPHABET

J, K, L

Name: _____

Trace each letter.

LETTERS
J K L

J ⌐⌐
K ⌐⌐⌐
L ⌐⌐

Hi!

Color in each box when you complete the activity.

1 Introduction	2 Jj	3 Kk	4 Ll
5 Match & Write	6 Color & Match	7 Graph	8 Review

31

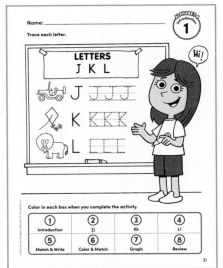

Name: _____ 2

Trace, then write.

J J J J J J J J

J J J J J J J J J

Color each picture that begins with the J sound.

Circle each J and j.

Juggle!

J I J J
j i T t

32

Name: _____ 3

Trace, then write.

K K K K K K K K

k k k k k k k k k

Color each picture that begins with the K sound.

Circle each K and k.

Key!

K k T K K
k h R k f

33

Name: _____ 4

Trace, then write.

L L L L L L L L

Color each picture that begins with the L sound.

Circle each L and l.

Ladybug!

t L T L l
L l f E l

34

Name: _____ 5

Draw lines!

Match each picture to the letter it begins with.

Jj
Kk
Ll

Write the missing letters.

J , K, L   j, k, l
j, k , l   J, K , L
J, K, L   j , k, l

35

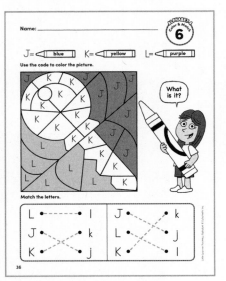

Name: _____ 6

J = blue   K = yellow   L = purple

Use the code to color the picture.

What is it?

Match the letters.

L • • l   J • • k
J • • k   L • • j
K • • j   K • • l

36

Name: _____ 7

Count and graph the letters.

Say each letter!

k   j   l
J L   K
j   l   k   j
K   L

J	j	K	k	L	l
4					
3					
2					
1					

37

Name: _____ 8

Fill in the letters. Color the pictures.

Great work! Bye!

J K L

L is for
J is for
K is for

Write the first letter for each word.

J k l

k ing   l eaf   j et

38

90

Little Learner Packets: Alphabet © Scholastic Inc.

PACKET 5

ALPHABET

M, N, O

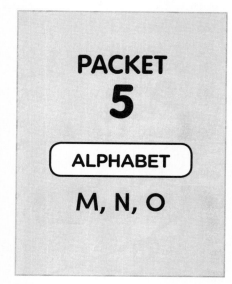

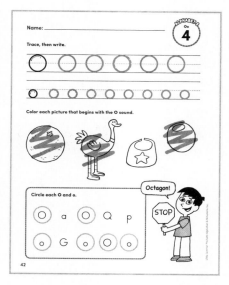

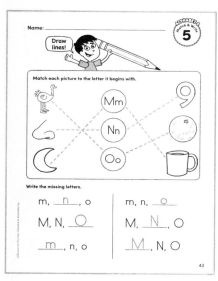

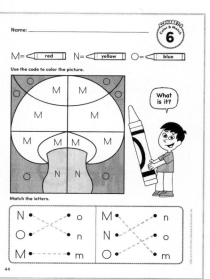

PACKET
6

ALPHABET

P, Q, R

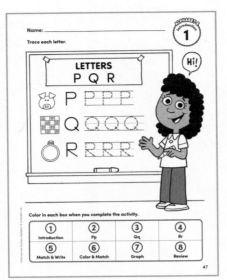

Name: _____

Trace each letter.

LETTERS
P Q R

P P P P
Q Q Q Q
R R R R

"Hi!"

Color in each box when you complete the activity.

| 1 Introduction | 2 Pp | 3 Qq | 4 Rr |
| 5 Match & Write | 6 Color & Match | 7 Graph | 8 Review |

47

Name: _____

Trace, then write.

P P P P P P P P P

p p p p p p p p p

Color each picture that begins with the P sound.

Circle each P and p.

P q a B P
p R P p b

"Popcorn!"

48

Name: _____

Trace, then write.

Q Q Q Q Q Q

q q q q q q q q

Color each picture that begins with the Q sound.

SHHH

Circle each Q and q.

O p Q q Q
q D q b Q

"Quarter!"

49

Name: _____

Trace, then write.

R R R R R R R R

r r r r r r r r r

Color each picture that begins with the R sound.

Circle each R and r.

R P r R r
n R m F r

"Rocket!"

50

Name: _____

"Draw lines!"

Match each picture to the letter it begins with.

Pp
Qq
Rr

Write the missing letters.

P , Q, R   p, q, _r_
p , q , _r_   P, _Q_, R
P, Q, _R_   _p_ , q , r

51

Name: _____

P = orange   Q = brown   R = green

Use the code to color the picture.

R	R	Q	R	R
R	P	P	P	R
R	P	P	P	R
R	P	P	P	R
R	P	P	P	R
R	R	P	R	R

"What is it?"

Match the letters.

P • → • q   R • → • q
R • → • p   P • ✕ • p
Q • → • r   Q • → • r

52

Name: _____

Count and graph the letters.

"Say each letter!"

P q R r
Q P p r
R Q P R
R q r q
Q

	P	p	Q	q	R	r
4						
3						
2						
1						

53

Name: _____

"Great work! Bye!"

Fill in the letters. Color the pictures.

P
Q
R

_R_ is for (rose)
_Q_ is for (quilt)
_P_ is for (pig)

Write the first letter for each word.

p
q
r

_p_ot   _r_ake   _q_ueen

54

PACKET 7

ALPHABET

S, T, U

Name: _____

Trace each letter.

LETTERS S T U

Hi!

S
T
U

Color in each box when you complete the activity.

| 1 Introduction | 2 Ss | 3 Tt | 4 Uu |
| 5 Match & Write | 6 Color & Match | 7 Graph | 8 Review |

55

Name: _____

Trace, then write.

S S S S S S S S

s s s s s s s s s

Color each picture that begins with the S sound.

Circle each S and s.

S P s g S
p R s S s

Sandwich!

56

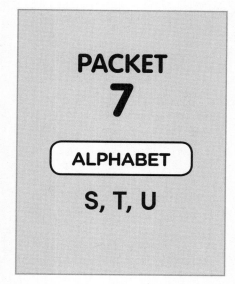

Name: _____

Trace, then write.

T

t

Color each picture that begins with the T sound.

Circle each T and t.

T k T t I
L t h T t

Toothbrush!

57

Name: _____

Trace, then write.

U U U U U U U U

u u u u u u u u u

Color each picture that begins with the U sound.

Circle each U and u.

u U V w U
W u U v U

Umbrella!

58

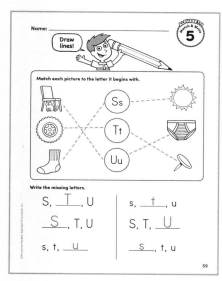

Name: _____

Draw lines!

Match each picture to the letter it begins with.

Ss
Tt
Uu

Write the missing letters.

S, _T_, U | s, _t_, u
_S_, T, U | S, T, _U_
s, t, _u_ | _s_, t, u

59

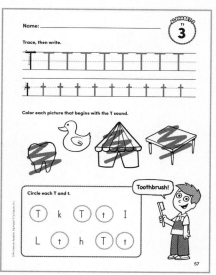

Name: _____

S = yellow   T = green   U = blue

Use the code to color the picture.

What is it?

Match the letters.

U • • u
T • • s
S • • t

S • • t
U • • s
T • • u

60

Name: _____

Count and graph the letters.

Say each letter!

T T s u
s s u t
u t
T U
s s s

S	s	T	t	U	u
4					
3					
2					
1					

61

Name: _____

Great work! Bye!

Fill in the letters. Color the pictures.

S T U

_T_ is for
_S_ is for
_U_ is for

Write the first letter for each word.

s t u

_s_ un   _u_ p   _t_ ent

62

93

PACKET 8

ALPHABET

V, W, X

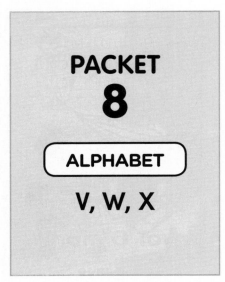

Name: _____

Trace each letter.

LETTERS
V W X

V VVV
W WWW
X XXX

Hi!

Color in each box when you complete the activity.

| ① Introduction | ② Vv | ③ Ww | ④ Xx |
| ⑤ Match & Write | ⑥ Color & Match | ⑦ Graph | ⑧ Review |

63

Name: _____

Trace, then write.

V V V V V V V V

V V V V V V V V

Color each picture that begins with the V sound.

Circle each V and v.

V k V v V

W v A w v

Vine!

64

3

Name: _____

Trace, then write.

W W W W W W

W W W W W W W W

Color each picture that begins with the W sound.

Circle each W and w.

w W v X W

x A w W w

Wig!

65

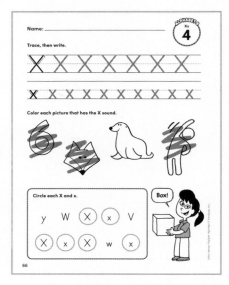

Name: _____

Trace, then write.

X X X X X X X

X X X X X X X X

Color each picture that has the X sound.

Circle each X and x.

y W X x V

X x X w x

Box!

66

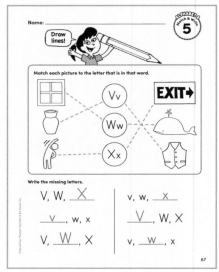

Name: _____

Draw lines!

Match each picture to the letter that is in that word.

Vv

Ww

Xx

EXIT→

Write the missing letters.

V, W, X | v, w, x

_V_, w, x | _V_, W, X

V, _W_, X | v, _w_, x

67

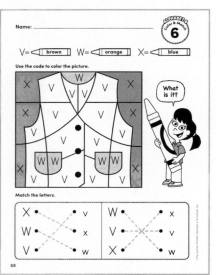

Name: _____

V=⊏ brown   W=⊏ orange   X=⊏ blue

Use the code to color the picture.

What is it?

Match the letters.

X • • v   W • • x
W • • x   V • ⨯ • v
V • • w   X • • w

68

Name: _____

Count and graph the letters.

Say each letter!

V w X
x x X
x W x
V v x

	V	v	W	w	X	x
4						
3						
2						
1						

69

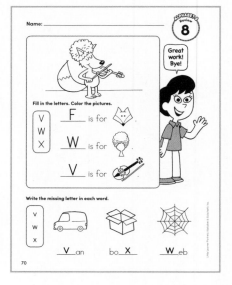

Name: _____

Great work! Bye!

Fill in the letters. Color the pictures.

| V W X |

_F_ is for

_W_ is for

_V_ is for

Write the missing letter in each word.

| v w x |

_V_an   bo_X_   _W_eb

70

94

PACKET 9

ALPHABET

Y, Z, Alphabet Review

Name: _____

ALPHABET 9 — Introduction — 1

Trace each letter.

LETTERS
Y Z

Hi!

Y

Z

Color in each box when you complete the activity.

| ① Introduction | ② Yy | ③ Zz | ④ Match & Write |
| ⑤ Color & Match | ⑥ Graph | ⑦ Review | ⑧ Alphabet Review |

71

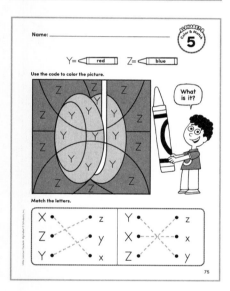

Name: _____

ALPHABET 9 — Yy — 2

Trace, then write.

Y Y Y Y Y Y Y Y

Y Y Y Y Y Y Y Y

Color each picture that begins with the Y sound.

Circle each Y and y.

Y v W Y y
y V x y Y

Yo-yo!

72

Name: _____

ALPHABET 9 — Zz — 3

Trace, then write.

Z Z Z Z Z Z Z Z

Z Z Z Z Z Z Z Z Z

Color each picture that begins with the Z sound.

ZOO

Circle each Z and z.

z H T Z z
x Z z w Z

Zero!

73

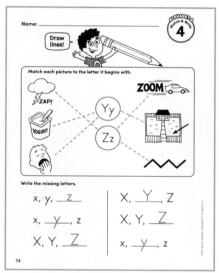

Name: _____

ALPHABET 9 — Match & Write — 4

Draw lines!

Match each picture to the letter it begins with.

ZAP!

YOGURT

ZOOM

Yy

Zz

Write the missing letters.

x, y, _Z_

x, _Y_, z

X, Y, _Z_

X, _Y_, Z

x, Y, _Z_

x, _Y_, z

74

Name: _____

ALPHABET 9 — Color & Math — 5

Y = red   Z = blue

Use the code to color the picture.

What is it?

Match the letters.

X • • z
Z • • y
Y • • x

Y • • z
X • • x
Z • • y

75

Name: _____

ALPHABET 9 — Graph — 6

Count and graph the letters.

Say each letter!

y z x
x z y y
Y y z z
z x Y y

	X	x	Y	y	Z	z
4						
3						
2						
1						

76

Name: _____

ALPHABET 9 — Review — 7

Almost done!

Fill in the letters. Color the pictures.

Y   _Y_ is for

Z   _Z_ is for

Write the first letter for each word.

y
z

_Z_oo   _Y_arn   _Z_ip

77

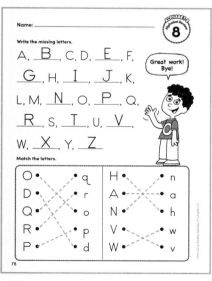

Name: _____

ALPHABET 9 — Alphabet Review — 8

Write the missing letters.

A, _B_, C, D, _E_, F,

G, _H_, _I_, J, K,

L, M, _N_, O, _P_, Q,

_R_, S, _T_, u, _V_,

W, _X_, Y, _Z_

Great work! Bye!

Match the letters.

O • • q
D • • r
Q • • o
R • • p
P • • d

H • • n
A • • a
N • • h
V • • w
W • • v

78

PACKET 10

ALPHABET

Alphabet Fun Pack

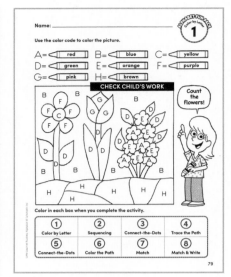

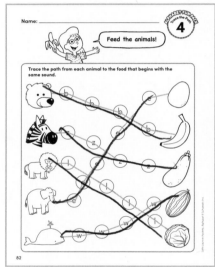

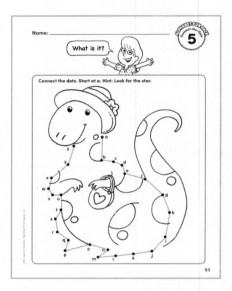

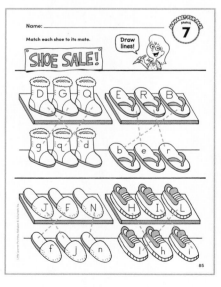

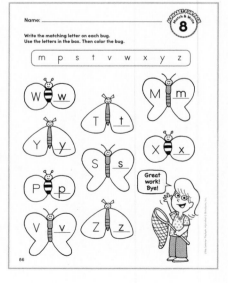

96